A PET WHAT?!

MY PET FERRET

BY PAIGE V. POLINSKY

BELLWETHER MEDIA • MINNEAPOLIS, MN

Action and adventure collide in EPIC.
Plunge into a universe of powerful
beasts, hair-raising tales, and high-speed
excitement. Astonishing explorations await.
Can you handle it?

This edition first published in 2020 by Bellwether Media, Inc.

No part of this publication may be reproduced in whole or in part without written permission of the publisher.
For information regarding permission, write to Bellwether Media, Inc., Attention: Permissions Department,
6012 Blue Circle Drive, Minnetonka, MN 55343.

Library of Congress Cataloging-in-Publication Data

Names: Polinsky, Paige V., author.
Title: My pet ferret / Paige V. Polinsky.
Description: Minneapolis, MN : Bellwether Media, 2020. | Series: A pet
   what?! | Includes bibliographical references and index. | Audience: Ages
   7-12. | Audience: Grades 4-6. | Summary: "Engaging images accompany
   information about pet ferrets. The combination of high-interest subject
   matter and light text is intended for students in grades 2 through 7"¬
   Provided by publisher.
Identifiers: LCCN 2019034493 (print) | LCCN 2019034494 (ebook) | ISBN
   9781644871812 (library binding) | ISBN 9781618918673 (ebook)
Subjects: LCSH: Ferrets as pets–Juvenile literature. | Ferret–Juvenile
   literature.
Classification: LCC SF459.F47 P65 2020 (print) | LCC SF459.F47 (ebook) |
   DDC 636.976/628–dc23
LC record available at https://lccn.loc.gov/2019034493
LC ebook record available at https://lccn.loc.gov/2019034494

Editor: Betsy Rathburn   Designer: Josh Brink

Printed in the United States of America, North Mankato, MN.

TABLE OF CONTENTS

TIME TO PLAY

Two little ferrets dash across the floor.
They race around in a furry flash!

Ferrets are **mammals**. They are part of the **weasel** family. They are also playful pets!

Ferrets have pointy faces and furry tails. Their slim bodies are long and bendy.

Ferrets grow up to 18 inches (46 centimeters) long. These pets are known for their strong **odor**.

FERRET PROFILE

- **Animal Type:** mammal
- **Life Span:** 6 to 10 years
- **Length:** 14 to 18 inches (36 to 46 centimeters)
- **Weight:** up to 5 pounds (2 kilograms)

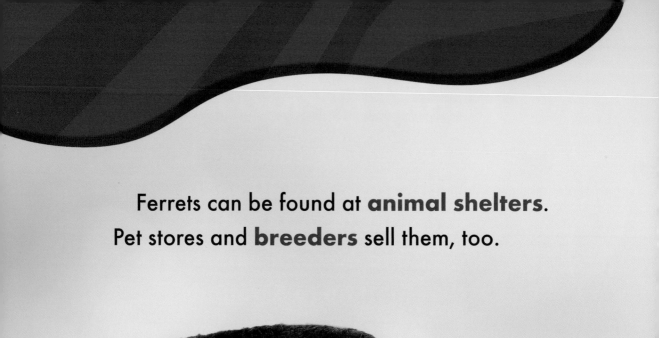

Ferrets can be found at **animal shelters**.
Pet stores and **breeders** sell them, too.

black-footed
ferret

But ferrets are banned in some places. Owners must know the laws in their area.

CLEAN AND COZY

Ferrets are happiest in pairs or groups. They need fresh air and room to play. Large wire cages make good homes. But they must shut tight. Ferrets are escape artists!

FERRET CAGE

water bottle

food bowl

toys

hammock

litter pan

bedding

Ferrets need cozy sleeping spots in their cages. **Hammocks** work great. Soft **bedding** lets ferrets **burrow**.

TIME TO NAP

Ferrets often sleep 18 hours a day!

hammock

litter pan

Litter pans help keep cages clean.
Owners should scoop them every day.
They should wash the whole cage every week.

Ferrets are **carnivores**. They need full bowls of dry ferret food. Bits of cooked meat or egg are tasty treats.

Fresh water should always be near.
Bottles or sturdy bowls are best. Ferrets
love to splash!

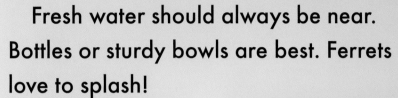

GONE IN A FLASH

Ferrets can wiggle
through holes as
small as 1 inch
(3 centimeters) wide!

NEEDY SWEETIES

Ferrets clean themselves. But they still need baths and nail trims. They need their fur and teeth brushed, too.

Vet visits are also important. **Cancer** is common in these pets.

FERRET HEALTH SUPPLIES

nail clippers

ferret shampoo

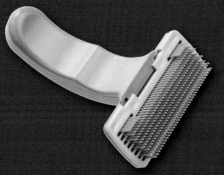

soft brush

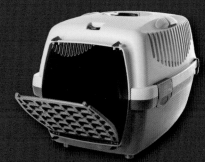

travel carrier for vet visits

treats for vet visits

Ferrets need hours of play out of their cages.
Owners must watch them closely.
These silly critters hop and dance with humans.
They can walk on leashes and even learn tricks!

FERRET CARE DUTIES

Daily
- ☑ fill food dish
- ☑ change water
- ☑ scoop litter pan
- ☑ brush fur
- ☑ play outside of cage

Weekly
- ☑ wash toys and bedding
- ☑ scrub cage

Monthly
- ☑ bathe
- ☑ brush teeth
- ☑ trim nails
- ☑ clean ears

As Needed
- ☑ bring to vet

Ferrets love to dig and climb. Hard toys
are best for their strong teeth.

These playful critters are hard work.
But they are fun pets if you can keep up!

21

GLOSSARY

animal shelters—places that take in animals whose owners cannot care for them

bedding—a soft material used to line animal cages

breeders—people who keep and take care of animals to produce more

burrow—to dig tunnels or holes to live in

cancer—an illness caused by cells that spread to one or many parts of the body

carnivores—animals that only eat meat

hammocks—beds made of cloth hung between two posts

litter pans—pans filled with dry material used as indoor toilets for animals

mammals—warm-blooded animals that have backbones and feed their young milk

odor—smell

weasel—any of a family of small, meat-eating animals that can hunt animals larger than themselves

TO LEARN MORE

AT THE LIBRARY

Bennett, Mia. *Ferrets.* New York, N.Y.: PowerKids Press, 2018.

Hughes, Catherine. *Little Kids First Big Book of Pets.* Washington, D.C.: National Geographic Kids, 2018.

Marcos, Victoria. *My Favorite Pet: Ferrets.* Irvine, Calif.: Xist Publishing, 2018.

ON THE WEB

FACTSURFER

Factsurfer.com gives you a safe, fun way to find more information.

1. Go to www.factsurfer.com.

2. Enter "ferrets" into the search box and click 🔍.

3. Select your book cover to see a list of related web sites.

INDEX